Understanding the Emotional and Physical Effects of Grief

A GRIEFSTEPS GUIDE

www.griefsteps.com

adapted from Grief Steps®
by Brook Noel

CHAMPION PRESS, LTD.
FREDONIA, WISCONSIN

Copyright © 2004 Brook Noel

All rights reserved.

No part of this book shall be reproduced, stored, or transmitted by any means without written permission from the publisher. Although every precaution has been taken in the preparation of this book, the publisher and author assume no responsibility for errors or omissions. Neither is any liability assumed for damages resulting from the use of the
information contained herein. For more information contact: Champion Press, Ltd., 4308 Blueberry Road, Fredonia WI 53021, www.championpress.com

Reasonable care has been taken in the preparation of the text to insure its clarity and accuracy. The book is sold with the understanding that the author and publisher are not engaged in rendering professional service.

The author and publisher specifically disclaim any liability, loss or risk, personal or otherwise, which is incurred as a consequence, directly or indirectly, of the use and application of any of the contents of this book.

ISBN: 1891400770
LCCN: 2004110031

Manufactured in the United States of America 10 9 8 7 6 5 4

Contents

4 / Important Notes
5 / Introduction: Basic Guidelines for Grief Work
7 / Chapter One: Getting Started
14 / Chapter Two: The Emotions of Grief
41 / Chapter Three: Understanding Emotional Triggers
47 / Chapter Four: Tools for Exploring Your Emotions
56 / Online Support Groups, Classes and Resources

Important Notes

Journaling: While reading this book, I recommend you keep a blank book or journal hand. There will suggestions for further writing. You will also uncover many emotions. Having a readily available source for recording your thoughts and emotions will help greatly during the grieving process.

Hope Notes: Throughout this guide you will see HOPE NOTES. These HOPE NOTES contain nuggets of wisdom or suggestions that should be carefully considered and contemplated during your healing process.

Online Support: References are periodically made to the Grief Steps® online support group. You can learn more about this group at www.griefsteps.com

Professional Help: If at any point you fear you may do harm to yourself or someone around you, seek professional help immediately or contact your local emergency response service.

Introduction
Basic Guidelines for Grief Work

Before we begin our journey, I want to outline some basic concepts to keep in mind as you work through the many emotions you will feel during grief. Read through these periodically. These statements will remind you to be patient and soft with yourself. Grief is never easy, but we need to be easy on ourselves.

I will be patient with myself and understand that grief often involves moving one step forward and two steps back.

I will reach out to others for help when I need support.

I will avoid abusing substances as a way to temporarily minimize my pain.

I will care for myself physically.

I will not isolate myself from friends, hobbies and activities.

I will avoid making major life decisions until I have worked through my grief.

I will grieve in my own time and not by how others think I should grieve.

I will create the space and time to honor my emotions.

I will understand that grief recovery takes time, and commit to healing—even if relief occurs slower than I would like.

I will remember that moving through grief often involves feeling painful and intense emotions.

I will remember that when I complete my grief work successfully, I can have a rich, although different, life.

Chapter One
Getting Started

"Problems do not go away. They must be worked through or else they remain, forever a barrier to the growth and development of the spirit." ~ M. Scott Peck

Often at the time of loss, we are simply incapable of comprehending or coping with our emotions. Then, as life beckons, we push our feelings aside or bury them within. Days, months and sometimes years drift by. We feel a gnawing sadness, but aren't sure of its source—or what to do about it. We know it is dark and ugly so we try to avoid it—often staying as far away from our emotions as possible. Some of us are scared that if we dig into that darkness, we might never come out.

However, we should be just as afraid of what happens when we don't dig into that darkness. When we leave it there to fester, it becomes the budding ground for our future. Everything we experience must pass through that pile before blossoming.

The process is somewhat like a root canal. We don't want to experience the pain of the root canal, but we don't want to experience the continuing pain of the toothache, either. The only way to obtain lasting comfort is by undergoing the pain of the root canal. To get past the pain, we must move through it. There simply isn't any other way.

For some, this process moves relatively quickly. It's as if a dam has burst and long-suppressed emotions flood forth. For others, the process may require a chisel, to chip away at the wall built within.

As you explore your emotions you may find the help of a support group or a professional extremely valuable. Or you may choose a close friend, pastor, or online support site such as www.griefsteps.com, to share your excavating process. And by all means, if at any point you fear you might inflict harm on yourself or others, seek professional help immediately.

I have always had a difficult time expressing my emotions. I can write about other peoples' feelings and express emotions on paper—but when it comes to verbalizing my own feelings, I often can't find the words. I remember one particular therapist's frustration peaking when he asked me for the fifth time, "How do you feel?" My response was the same as my first four, "I don't know!"

What I learned is that "I don't know" often equals "I don't want to know." We may not want to know what we feel because it scares us. We may not want to know how we feel because then we are responsible for doing something about it.

I am an upbeat and optimistic person. I didn't want to feel the sadness of loss. I felt it would reduce my productivity and affect how I cared for my family. I didn't want people to see me sad. I didn't want anyone to see me weak. But when it comes to grief, ignorance is never bliss. There cannot be bliss again until we have dug out of the darkness of "not feeling."

Later, we will look at some specific tools to use when facing your emotions. For now, let's look at the different emotions that often travel with grief.

> ***Hope Note:*** *When we answer the question, "How do I feel?" with "I don't know," it may mean "I don't want to know." Owning our emotions requires us to take responsibility. This responsibility is the only way to move forward in our healing.*

Depression and Anxiety

As you work through your grief, it is important to monitor yourself and the stages you are going through. It's important to remember that the psychiatric profession has advanced by leaps and bounds over the past decades. Many doctors are very adept at dealing with emotional and cognitive disorders—from anxiety to depression. Many people have sought professional help with successful results.

Hope Note: If you think you might benefit from professional help or medication, at least make an appointment for assessment and learn about your options. Doing so is not a sign of weakness, but a sign of strength. It shows that you are strong enough to deal with your problems—versus brushing them beneath the surface.

One piece of advice: make sure you feel comfortable with the professional you choose to work with. You should be able to ask questions without feeling rushed. You should feel your questions are answered completely and thoroughly. You should feel that your provider has a genuine interest in what you are saying and is helping you to comprehend and process your grief. If you are the least bit uncomfortable after one or two visits, request a different professional (if others are available at the practice) or call a different service. These are very personal issues that you are dealing with. It is imperative that you feel comfortable, safe and heard. It is not uncommon to go through several providers before you find someone you "connect" with.

> ***Hope Note:*** *I will remember that when I complete my grief work successfully, I can have a rich, although different, life.*

Healthy Grieving vs. Unhealthy Grieving

In the table on page 9, I have listed examples of healthy and unhealthy grieving. As you work through the grief process, refer to this chart periodically. Note which statements describe you. If you repeatedly find yourself grieving in unhealthy ways, seek the help of a support group or professional for guidance in your grief work.

Healthy Grieving	Unhealthy Grieving
Although saddened, you communicate honestly with friends and family.	Avoiding friends and family for a prolonged period of time (over three weeks).
You tend to your basic self-case needs.	You are not eating well, sleeping well or tending to your basic self-care needs.
You have accepted the reality of your loss.	You are in denial about your loss or still trying to "go back in time" and change the outcome.
Although you may occasionally have a self-destructive thought, it passes quickly and the majority of your focus is on moving forward.	You have persistent, obsessive or strong self-destructive thoughts. (Seek help immediately.)
You have discovered healthy outlets for your anger.	You take your anger out on yourself or those people close to you. (Seek help immediately.)
You realize that your world has changed and are sad about this change, but are open to what it may bring.	You have become immobilize by depression and cannot see hope for the future. (Seek help immediately.)
You are facing your feelings.	You are masking your feelings through self-medication.

Chapter Two
The Emotions of Grief

Anger

Anger can be directed at others, yourself, society in general, the world, religion or any other source that you hold responsible for your loss. Anger often stems from blame. When we feel things could be different had "X" not happened, we feel anger toward "X". When we can't find someone or something to hold accountable for our pain, anger may point itself toward our faith or the world at large. Sometimes, it turns inward, becoming self-destructive.

Let's examine the types of anger that are natural, though unhealthy. This wisdom is based on the work of psychotherapist Pamela D. Blair, Ph.D., in the book that we co-authored of *I Wasn't Ready to Say Goodbye*.

Some of us will express anger when we are not getting the support we need from friends, family or work. While intensely wrapped in our grief, we usually don't think to ask for support. Instead we lash out at those close to us with hostility, irritability and anger. If we can recognize this anger for what it is, we can use it in a healthy way. This can be our cue that we need to strengthen our support networks. In some instances, people may be offering support but we are not in an accepting mode. In those times we need to look within. Still at other times, people may be offering support but it might not be the type of support we need. No one is a mind-reader. If our support-needs are going unmet we need to communicate our needs to those trying to help.

Displaced anger is simply misdirected anger. We want someone to take responsibility for what has happened. We need someone to blame and to be held accountable. We may scream or yell at those we feel could have influenced the outcome of this life-loss-chapter. Displaced anger is completely natural and will lessen as we acknowledge what has happened. However, if you ever feel your anger is motivating you to harm someone, or is becoming an obsession for revenge, you should seek immediate help.

Anger can also surface when we recall past moments of turmoil, pain or unresolved issues within our terminated relationship with the person we have lost. Suddenly we are forced to realize the reality of our separation. When that happens, memories flood through. Within these memories there are bound to be recollections of feisty exchanges, arguments and past hurts. We may over-criticize ourselves for unresolved conflicts in our past. It is unrealistic, however, to expect perfection in any relationship. Immersing ourselves in the "should haves" and "could haves" of the past will only prevent us from dealing effectively with our anger in the present, moving on, and ultimately letting go."

To understand your anger, try making a list of the "should haves" and "could haves" that you recite repeatedly to yourself. Include those you feel you personally "should have done" as well as the "should haves" and "could haves" for other people involved in your loss.

Anger also occurs when we suppress our feelings. Anger is not the most accepted emotion in today's culture. In fact, some people don't even recognize anger as part of the grieving process. Depending on our support network and situation, we may be encouraged not to show our anger. When this happens, the anger still exists and needs to be released, so it is released inward, usually with corresponding guilt. This can cause a variety of problems. We may become sick, depressed, have chronic pain or begin having nightmares. Discovering healthy ways to release our anger is important for healing.

Appropriate anger is the point that we all hope to get to eventually. In this phase we can take our anger, in whatever form, and vent it. There are many ways to release anger appropriately. Here are a few… place a checkmark next to any that you think would be helpful to you. Try one of these exercises the next time you find yourself upset and ridden with anger.

- Beat a pillow
- Create a sacred space where you can go and not be heard or seen to let the anger out of your system
- Use journaling to record and release your angry feelings
- Accept that anger is not bad—but staying angry is unhealthy. We learn to accept that fact by feeling our anger and allowing it to pass, instead of taking root.
- Take a walk out into an unpopulated area and scream until you are exhausted
- Talk with a friend, therapist or counselor
- Have a good cry, let the tears flow

Hope Note: *Choose several healthy outlets for your anger and record them in your journal.*

Of all the emotions, anger is the most difficult to deal with. We live in a society where anger is frowned upon. Anger scares people. Anger indicates that we are "out of control." Angry people are often labeled "bad people." However there is a big difference between an angry person and a person who is feeling their anger. The latter is a temporary state—not a permanent one. But, when we don't allow our anger the opportunity to pass through us, it takes hold and we experience life through an angry lens of distortion. We might be outwardly angry and loud—or we may be quietly angry. We look happy and nice most of the time—but then we give someone a little jab here or a little jab there. Or we might become bitter, which is the debilitating cousin to anger.

The question becomes: how do we honor and feel our anger in a world where anger is considered "bad"? We accept that anger is not bad—only staying angry is. We must learn to accept that by feeling our anger and allowing it to pass, we are letting it go instead of letting it take root. We must learn to make space to honor our emotions—the good, the bad and the ugly, with the hope of moving forward.

Anxiety

Anxiety is a sense of nervousness, edginess or agitation, often without a readily identifiable source. Sometimes it is attached to an event that we consider difficult or dangerous, like driving in a strange city, or facing an unknown future. We feel our heart race, our palms sweat and a general sense of unease. At its worst, anxiety turns into a panic attack where our breathing is stifled and we may feel like we are having a heart attack.

Anxiety is often accompanied by additional emotions—fear, anger, sadness—it tends to travel with a partner. When we feel anxious, the most important thing we can do is pinpoint the cause, take a deep breath and conduct a "reality check."

Begin by asking yourself, "What do I feel anxious about?" Say your answer aloud or write it down. Continue asking yourself this question until you find an answer that carries some "zing" to it. You'll know in your gut when you have stumbled on the true source of your anxiety. Often, you'll have to ask yourself this question several times to get to the true source.

Once you have uncovered the true source, write it down on a piece of paper. Beneath your sentence write down the "fact and fiction" about your statement. For example, if you have written, "I feel anxious about driving in a big city because I think I will get into an accident," write down what reality supports your statement and what doesn't. If you have driven in the city before, and were not in an accident, that would be a strike against your anxiety. If you took your time, wore your seat-belt and had a good map, those would be a few more strikes against your anxiety. Continue looking for "faults" in your anxiety. This exercise can often decrease or eliminate our anxiety altogether.

Hope Note: When we feel anxious, the most important thing we can do is pinpoint the cause, take a deep breath and conduct a "reality check."

As unfair and as unjust as life can be, it always offers us a choice. Remember that 98% of what we worry about never happens. Living in a state of perpetual worry is a terrible way to live life. If you find yourself constantly riddled by anxiety, you will need an arsenal of cognitive exercises to begin to loosen anxiety's hold. You may also want to consult a professional to see if you have General Anxiety Disorder. This disorder is quite prevalent in today's hectic world and there are supportive systems in place to help those who are suffering its grip.

Bitterness

I can best describe bitterness as a shadow that will not lift. It is a cloud that casts its dark color on our every thought and action, constantly reminding us of how unjust life can be. Those of you who feel it, recognize this emotion easily. It's that abyss that is always a step away and that follows us no matter how fast we run.

Bitterness is caused by an incomplete grieving cycle. When we don't do our grief work and find conclusive meaning; when we don't accept responsibility; when we don't reconcile ourselves to our loss and relevant reality, bitterness sweeps over our life.

Some bitterness is to be expected as we work through our grief, but in the end, it should not be a predominant state in which we continue to live. Those who face each day with a "chip on their shoulder" are examples of people who have chosen to let bitterness take control.

> **Hope Note:** *As unfair and as unjust as life can be, it always offers us a choice.*

In our times of loss we have the choice to grow or to wilt. No one can make the choice for us—we are each responsible for how we choose to live our lives. It may seem impossible to choose to live a good life after the loss we have experienced. That is simply a sign that you are not far enough along in your grief work. When you grieve healthily, choosing higher ground becomes the easy choice—staying stuck the difficult one.

That doesn't mean that at the end of our grief work life will come up roses—surely, I am not that naive. Life will always be different. Life will always be bittersweet. But life remains the greatest gift we are given, and the greatest way to accept that gift is to live it...not to fall victim to it.

Blame

Although blame is more an action than an emotion, I feel it appropriate to address here. Blame is dangerous. When we sit with blame, we give ourselves an excuse not to move forward. Everything is someone else's fault. Our pain, our sadness, our depression—it's all someone else's doing.

"If only" are two words uttered over and over again when we are stuck in the blame game. Instead of moving forward, we recount the ways our life could be different "if only" something would or wouldn't have happened. Blame becomes anger's "scape goat."

Blame is a mask. When you take it off, you often see fear. Fear to feel our emotions, fear to go inside and dig through the darkness. Or you may see anger and unforgiveness. When we feel angry we don't have to think ahead toward hope. We don't have to plan for the future—because our future remains at the hands of someone or something else.

Through blame, we can seemingly skip the parts of life we don't want to face and page forward to something else. Or we can page backward and recant the "if only's" of a past we cannot change.

When we get stuck in the blame game we halt our grief work. We can attempt to move forward but the game will always be waiting for us. Moving through blame is much like moving through anxiety.

First, we write down who we blame and for what. Sometimes we blame ourselves. No matter whom or what it is, write it down or say it aloud. Then write down the evidence you have to support your claim.

As we do this, we quickly see whether our blame is founded or unfounded. If we find that reality does not support our blame, we can then begin to let that blame go. Each time we repeat the feeling we can dig for another fact that demonstrates its untruth.

Sometimes, our blame is justified. Perhaps someone we loved developed lung cancer because they smoked cigarettes. We may blame them for the illness. Perhaps someone we loved was killed by a drunk driver. We may blame the person who drank. These cases have a solid argument for blame. In these cases, we need to move forward toward forgiveness—to let go of the blame that keeps us from healing.

Blame, like guilt, doesn't hurt anyone but the beholder. By choosing to hold onto blame you are tightening its grip on your life.

Detachment

Detachment is another common step in our grief work. Usually when we experience the shock of our loss, we temporarily detach from the world around us. It is too hard to face our loss, so our body shuts down, closing out reality. If we move through our grief work successfully, little by little we reopen ourselves to reality until we fully rejoin society. When we don't successfully complete our grief work, we remain in a state of detachment where we continue to withdraw from people, hobbies, events and feelings.

Sometimes, ironically, detachment takes the form of attachment to something else. In order to detach from our feelings and our pain, we attach ourselves to work, a hobby, a substance—something to occupy us other than the pain we feel inside, providing a way to avoid rather than address forgiveness.

How can you tell if you are in a state of detachment? Have you abandoned the majority of the friends you had before your loss? If so, you are in a state of detachment. If you were asked, "How do you feel?" and could not answer, you are in a state of detachment. Have you given up hobbies you enjoyed before your loss? If yes, you are in a state of detachment—all leading to emotional withdrawal.

Life does cycle and change, and this does not mean that we should hold onto everything. Often when we experience a loss, we lose other pieces of our lives, as well. For example, if we have become widowed, we may lose friends that we used to engage with as couples. That is normal. Likewise, we may take a year or two break from an activity that we once had enjoyed as a couple. That too is normal. It is when we begin withdrawing from ALL, or the majority, of, specific life areas that we know we have not grieved successfully.

Why do we detach? Like many other coping mechanisms, we detach because we hope it will minimize our pain. If we don't associate with the people or events that remind us of our hurt, perhaps we can avoid our hurt all-together. However, continued detachment and emotional withdrawal will only postpone the process of healthy recovery.

Hope Note: Continued detachment and emotional withdrawal will only postpone the process of healthy recovery.

Fear

Throughout our grief work, fear can be debilitating. Some people experience fear in a small number of areas, while others become overwhelmed by fear. It is perfectly natural to be fearful. We have experienced a loss that cannot be prepared for. Common fears after a death can include fearing any situation that remotely resembles the way our loved one died. We might fear that others we love will die in the same way. We may fear our own death. We may fear that we will be unable to go on. We may fear that the simplest of activities will lead to repeated tragedy.

Fear serves several purposes. In the initial stages of grief it gives us something on which to focus besides our loss. It also offers potential control. For example, if someone we loved died in a car accident and now we fear that riding in a car could kill us, and choose not to ride in a car, we create the illusion of control. When we face such a substantial loss our lives and emotions whirl out of control. At first it is common to seek any sort of control measures that we can find. Most of the time, fear will run its course naturally. If you find your fear becoming debilitating, seek the help of a professional.

Guilt

Of all the blocks mentioned in this chapter, guilt may be the strongest of all. Struggling with the question, "Why did this happen to me, to my family, to my loved one?" can create so much anxiety, pain and self-doubt that you stay stuck in your grief, much longer and more intensely than needed.

We must remind ourselves that our goal is to overcome, and resume a healthy lifestyle full of meaning. Guilt won't let us do that. Many people experience Survivor's

Guilt after loss. Survivor's Guilt is characterized by a sense of feeling that we should not have survived a tragedy. We feel guilty when we feel happiness. We feel guilty for our joy. This guilt is a natural part of the grieving process. When we experience Survivor's Guilt, it can be helpful to write out how you feel. Then imagine the person you have lost commenting on your feelings. This often serves as a release since those we love would not want us to experience pain, guilt or other negative emotions.

We must remember that guilt is a useless emotion. It's like a glue that cements us to our pain and our past. We cannot move forward when shrouded with guilt. We must remind ourselves that our goal is to overcome our negative feelings and resume a healthy lifestyle full of meaning and hope. Harboring our guilt won't let us do that.

Process your guilt with a trusted friend, therapist, clergy person or through the journaling and releasing your feeling exercises found throughout this book.

Helplessness

Helplessness stems from not knowing our own power. When we underestimate or are detached from the miracles that we are, and the power we can exert, we feel helpless. We feel our lives moving forward and that we have little control over the process. We don't know how to cope or make decisions. We don't know how to get from Point A to Point B—sometimes we don't even know where Point A or Point B are.

Helplessness can also come from being stifled when life seems to pile one thing then another on top of us. The bigger the pile the more overwhelmed we become until our overwhelmed feelings transform to helplessness. Our loss and the grief that ensues can be so profound, we don't know where to start. And so we don't. As we remain inactive, the pile gets bigger, further propelling our sense of helplessness.

The way out of this vicious cycle begins by realizing that we do have a choice. We always have a choice. Our journey begins the day we make the choice to take our first step toward healing. Keep in mind I wrote step not leap. We take one little step at a time, honing our skills, until we emerge from our sense of helplessness, to arrive at the other side of grief.

Hopelessness

Of all the emotions, hopelessness can be the scariest. True hopelessness involves feeling that not only is the world unjust and unfair, but that it won't and can't change. Hopelessness is where people give up. They decide that they can never feel any better and it isn't worth the effort to try. Hopelessness like helplessness comes when we give up our power to choose.

Fortunately, like all of these difficult emotions, there is a way out of hopelessness. It can be the hardest emotion to work with since it is so deeply rooted. Convincing ourselves to try can be very difficult. Like other unhealthy emotions, hopelessness comes from unfinished grief work. When we don't complete our grieving process, and fail integrate our loss with our life, we become hopeless and unable to see any reason to carry on.

Hope Note: Understanding the emotions and physical affects of grief as presented in this book can help you work through unresolved grief and emotional difficulty. Take this first step... then another... then another... Yes, grief is a journey of 2000 miles, but as the Chinese proverb states, "it begins with a single step." You have already taken your first step by beginning this book. You are not totally hopeless—you believed enough to read this far. Let that be the first step. Now, keep reading, let that be the next.

Loneliness

Whenever we feel the need to reach out yet no one is there to reciprocate, loneliness ensues. Sometimes our loneliness is valid—we don't have access to the specific help that we desire. At other times loneliness is caused by our own choice not to reach out to others (unhealthy detachment).

Fortunately, loneliness is one of the emotions over which we have the most control. Thanks to the variety of support groups, the internet and our own personal circles, there is always someone that we can reach out to, if we gather the energy to do so.

In the case of loss, often our loneliness is a yearning for the person or thing that we have lost. While we can't replace the exact thing or person we have lost, we can work through our emptiness to try and understand the void. We can minimize the pain of our loneliness with healthy steps toward healing.

Numbness

When we face loss, it often feels like the world is moving by and around us while we are standing still. We are in a fog, a haze. Life can seem almost surreal. This is a state of numbness. Numbness arrives after the shock of learning about our loss. Our body and mind continue to shut down in an attempt to protect us from the harsh reality at hand. As we do our grief work this numbness fades.

When we don't complete our grief work, numbness continues to surround us. We lose touch with our feelings as we attempt to protect ourselves from the pain. A perpetual feeling of numbness serves as a clue that we are not dealing with our emotions, feelings and losses successfully. Consequently numbness can last for a long time.

Sadness and Depression

It is important to note that there is a difference between sadness and depression. While we grieve, we should expect to feel sadness. The intensity of this sadness will differ with the type of loss we are grieving. Shedding tears and being emotional often constitute sadness—not depression. If you find yourself immobilized, unable to concentrate, sleeping too much or too little, you are grieving, You will likely experience grief and sadness through the following traits (although these should be temporary):

- weakness and feeling drained
- loss of appetite
- extreme fatigue
- extreme irritability
- unresponsiveness
- inability to focus or concentrate
- feeling hopeless or powerless
- aches and pains
- lack of personal hygiene
- a feeling that the world is not a safe place

In her book *The Courage to Grieve*, Judy Tatelbaum writes, "So much of our energy is tied up inside that little energy is available for the action of functioning. We may be moody. At times we may feel pain and weep, and then at other times we may feel detached and without emotion. During this period we may be withdrawn and unable to relate to other people. Negativity, pessimism, emptiness and a temporary sense of meaninglessness of life are all symptoms of depression. 'What's the use?' or 'Why bother?' are typical feelings. We may be acutely restless and then become immobile. The essential thing to remember is that the pain of grief is never constant and does not last forever. Throughout this middle phase of mourning, the myriad of feelings of grief come and go in waves, with lessening intensity Any feelings we don't face will take root in our heart and color our world as time goes on."

"Lessening intensity" are the key words here. If you are progressing healthily you should notice these "symptoms" of grief subsiding. If these symptoms do not subside or begin to cause you physical or emotional harm, professional help is needed. If you are unsure if you are feeling depression or sadness, please seek the help of a professional for a diagnosis.

> ***Hope Note:*** *The essential thing to remember is that the pain of grief is never constant and does not last forever. Let the river of pain flow away from you, as you begin to recognize the currents of healing.*

Chapter Three
Understanding Emotional Triggers

It is not only important to understand what emotions we are feeling, it is also important to understand how these emotions affect us. It can be helpful to keep a journal documenting your "emotional triggers."

Cognitive experts have determined that what we think about creates our feelings, our feelings create our moods and our moods fuel our actions. In it's most basic sense the equation looks like this:

> Thoughts = feelings,
> which = moods, which = actions
> therefore   Thoughts = actions

When we work this equation in reverse, we can see where our actions stem from. First, take an action and ask yourself what type of mood you were in when you did it. Then ask yourself what feelings led to that mood. Lastly, ask yourself what thoughts you were feeling. This process may be tenuous at first, but the more often you do it, the easier it will become. This is an excellent way to get in touch with your thoughts and feelings, and to see how they affect your life.

Once you have done this exercise a few times, you will be able to recognize "triggers." When you recognize a thought process, you will know what mood and action it will lead to. Knowing this gives you the opportunity to change your thoughts and thus change the eventual action. This process is where the cliché, "Change your mind, change your life," stems from. Recognizing your personal "triggers" will help you gain control over actions and reactions.

Will I Ever Get Over It?

It is human nature to want to move away from, and avoid, pain. Facing our sadness and grief is complicated and often messy. We long to "rewind" to that place where we felt more complete. "How long will this go on?" ask many bereaved people. "Will this ever end?" The answer to that question rests with you. Will you do the grief work necessary to heal? Will you take the time to understand, process and work through it? If you choose not to do the work, you sentence yourself to a difficult and turbulent road ahead. Yet, if you choose to face and process your pain, you can move beyond it.

Moving beyond our pain does not mean that it will not resurface. Deep pain and sadness, as if our loss has just occurred, can surface at odd moments and without warning. Often, when we finally feel like we are moving forward or have had a few "good months," out of "nowhere" the sadness resurfaces, the disbelief, the flashback, the rage, the insane feeling, the sorrow.

Sometimes these "grief flashbacks" occur during dates and places that trigger reminders of your experience. It might be a holiday season with an empty chair at the table. Perhaps it is an anniversary, yet there is no one to celebrate with. Maybe a movie you saw with a loved one is released onto video and the display catches your eye as you walk through the store. Maybe your lost child loved Legos® and when you go through the local drive-thru the "toy of the month" features those colorful square blocks. Some of these situations we can prepare for or avoid, but there will always be the "ambush" with its unexpected "grief flashbacks" where the tears begin to flow and the outrage returns.

Recovery from loss is a lifetime process. It's true that the pain lessens with time, but expect to be ambushed by grief occasionally.

In a letter Sigmund Freud wrote to a man who lost his son, he stated, "Although we know that after such a loss the acute state of mourning will subside, we also know we shall remain inconsolable and will never find a substitute. No matter what may fill the gap, even if it be filled completely, it nevertheless remains something else. And actually this is how it should be. It is the only way of perpetuating that love which we do not want to relinquish."

Know that you can find happiness again, and that happiness can be intense. It will just be different. The way grief changes is conveyed well in Wendy Feiereisen's poem entitled, "Grief."

> You don't get over it
>   you just get through it
>
> you don't get by it
>   because you can't get around it
>
> it doesn't "get better"
>   it just gets different
>
> every day…
>   grief puts on a new face.

In Gay Hendricks workbook, *Learning to Love Yourself,* he offers another way to look at painful events and emotions. "…think of a painful feeling as being like a bonfire in a field. At first it is hot, unapproachable. Later it may still smolder. Even later, you can walk on the ground without pain, but you know there is an essence of the fire that still remains. Take your own time, but be sure to walk over the ground again. You must do so because whatever you run away from runs you."

Chapter Four
Tools for Exploring Your Emotions

Make A Space: If you're like me, you may find it helpful to schedule a "Vacation for Feeling." In order for me to truly get in touch with how I felt during my initial grieving, I had to make a safe space for the feelings to surface. My day-to-day life as a CEO and Mom is hectic and crazy, and doesn't allow me a single side-step. Only by taking several days away, with the sole intention of exposing my grief, was I then able to let my emotions rise to the surface. In the safety of my solitary hotel, I could feel my sadness. There was no one there to see me as "weak," and no one there that I had to care for. My only "roommate" was my grief.

Hope Note: *Where will you create a space for your grief?*

Develop 'Grief Sessions:' Grief Sessions are set times when you honor your feelings. In our busy days we tend to immerse ourselves in the activities of life (sometimes mindful, sometimes mindless) leaving us little time to work with our grief. But we can't get through what we do not feel and address.

Some people find success in spending an hour taking a walk and getting in touch with their grief, while others can sit outside with a journal and express their feelings. Just as our grief is unique, so will our sessions be. Write down some ideas for your own Grief Sessions—then schedule one on your calendar.

> *Hope Note: When and where will you hold your first Grief Session? Take the time to make a concrete appointment for yourself. You are worth it.*

Try Your Hand at Journaling: Writing about feelings has proven a successful venue for many people. When you write, don't worry about punctuation, grammar or how your writing might sound to another person. When you are writing, just aim to express your innermost thoughts. Write whatever comes to mind. Dig for words. Anything goes when journaling. You can keep your journal or burn your pages—whatever is most comfortable for you. I recommend keeping your journal as a chronicle of your journey. However, if several pages are extremely sensitive, you may choose to burn those pages or keep them in a password protected file on a computer; or if handwritten, under lock and key. You want your journal to be a private and secure place where you can confess your feelings without concern.

The actual physical act of "writing" can be very rewarding. It shows a respect and caring for ourselves, since we take the time to create a thoughtful letter that can be held and re-read. We are valuing our abstract thoughts by giving them a "physical existence." I have worked with many people who have found this process both cleansing and healing (even those people who swore they would never enjoy writing). Being able to look back on a collection of writing is encouraging—we see how far we have come.

If you have a difficult time starting to write, try listening to some emotional or moving music. Let the notes evoke your feelings and write about what you feel.

Using a "Sentence Starter" can also be helpful. Try writing "I feel..." and then completing the sentence. Continue doing that over and over. The more times you do this, the more the sentence-starter will reveal. Or you can use a sentence-starter that names an emotion, "I feel angry because..."

Try using some of the following "starters" in your own journaling:

I am sad because...
I am angry because...
I feel anxious about...
I am depressed about...
I feel lonely when...

I am scared that…
The hardest part is…
I miss…
I regret that…
I can't handle…
I wish I…

Hope Note: *Choose two sentence-starters from the list above and use them in your journaling today or tomorrow.*

Utilize Freewriting: Freewriting is the process of recording thoughts and feelings on the fly. Instead of analyzing what you are writing, or by worrying about form or structure, you just write continually. There are only two rules for freewriting—you can't stop moving your pen or pencil—and you can't erase anything you have written. The point of this exercise is to spontaneously dig past the surface and into your soul—giving your soul a space for open-ended expression. Freewriting works especially well for those who are intimidated by the thought of journaling, but it can also be used in conjunction with journaling. I recommend a 5-minute freewrite first thing in the morning. When we first wake, we can access our innermost thoughts more readily. If you are leery about trying a freewrite, that is all the more reason to push yourself to do so. You might find that this can help you uncover much of your inner life. Try to make a commitment to freewrite at least four mornings each week for five minutes. Set a timer for yourself. When the timer dings, stop writing.

Hope Note: Put down this book and try a five minute freewrite. Avoid excuses and just take action.

Identify Your Emotions: One of the most valuable skills we can gain during the grief journey is the ability to identify and understand our emotions. When we feel a gnawing sense of pain, we need to ask ourselves... "How do I feel?" With emotions buried or repressed, we often just know we feel "bad" but are unsure why. When we don't understand our feelings, it's like going to the doctor seeking treatment for pain, but when the doctor asks why we are there our response is merely... "Something hurts, but I'm not sure what." We could spend hours going back and forth to the doctor, but without an identified cause of the pain, and a clear diagnosis, the odds of successful treatment aren't good. Doctors ask us questions to help isolate and identify our pain. Once determined, a treatment can be selected. Grief work is very similar. We need to ask ourselves questions and identify our emotions so that we can "treat" them.

The next time you feel a gnawing pain, ask "What am I feeling?" Continue to ask this question of yourself, journaling your answers, until you stumble across the answer that feels intuitively "real." After you identify your feeling, you can take the next steps to help you move forward, understand and heal from the pain. Let your first steps toward healing lead to more steps forward, and then more, until you no longer fall victim to your pain. There is hope and you have taken the first steps toward that hope.

"What the caterpillar calls the end of the world, the master calls a butterfly." ~ **Richard Bach**

Online Support Classes, Groups and Resources

Take a step toward healing with interactive, online courses led by best-selling author Brook Noel

How do the classes work?
Its easy to get started with a GriefSteps class. Simply enroll in the class of your choice at www.griefsteps.com We offer a wide variety of classes ranging in price from $19 to $129.

What do I get with my class?
1. Once you enroll, you'll receive a welcome packet that will contain directions for the classes.

2. Each class has "assignments" that you can turn in for comments from Brook Noel.

3. Each class also has a message board where you can post questions and talk to other students.

4. There is also a designated weekly, one-hour "chat" time for each class. You can log on to the private chat to talk about your experiences and assignments. These chats are moderated by Brook Noel.

*Participate in chats, message boards and assignments is optional.

Healing Exercises – Part One
In this interactive, online course, you'll complete 10 different exercises that help you move forward through grief and resolve open issues. The exercises can be completed again and again after the class to further your healing. Brook Noel will comment on work you choose to turn in and encourage you in your journey.
Class length – 6 weeks   Cost $49

Now What? Living After Loss
This class offers a solid foundation for anyone wondering how to go on after loss. You'll learn what to expect physically and emotionally and how to take your first steps toward healing.
Class length – 3 weeks   Cost $19

Rituals to Honor Your Loved One
Rituals are a wonderful way to keep the memory of your loved one with you. This class will introduce you to different types of rituals and guide you in creating one of your own.
Class length – 4 weeks   Cost $29

When Will the Pain End? Working through Unresolved Grief
Throughout this 10 week course, you'll learn about the different stages of grief and how to recognize which of your life losses have not been grieved completely. You'll learn exercises and tactics to heal and work through unresolved grief, which are the most common causes of sadness and depression. This is the perfect class for anyone who is having difficulty moving forward after a life loss.
Class length – 10 weeks   Cost $99

The Healing Journey: Writing through Grief

In this writing-intensive class, you'll learn how to write the story of your loss and discover its meaning. You'll create a record of your cherished memories and discover how your loved one is still in your life today. When you complete this class you'll have a very special chronicle of you and your loved ones relationship.
Class length – 12 weeks   Cost $129

How to Create Your Own Support Group

In this class you will be given assignments that will lead to the creation of your own support group by the completion of the course. You'll decide what type of support group you want to start (online or in-person), create materials to help spread the word and learn how to successfully guide your support group meetings.
Class length – 8 weeks   Cost $79

Basic Strategies and Exercises for Healing

In this interactive, online course, you'll complete 4 different exercises that can help you on your grief journey. You'll also learn what to expect on your journey and strategies for coping.
Class length – 3 weeks   Cost $19

Take a step toward healing.
Enroll today at www.griefsteps.com

Grief Resources from Grief Steps®

I Wasn't Ready to Say Goodbye: Surviving, Coping and Healing After the Sudden Death of a Loved One by Pamela D. Blair, Ph.D. and Brook Noel (14.95) ISBN 1-891400-27-4; Companion Workbook also available (18.95) ISBN 1-891400-50-9

Grief Steps: 10 Steps to Regroup, Rebuild and Renew After Any Life Loss by Brook Noel ($14.95) ISBN 1-891400-35-5; Companion Workbook also available ($18.95) ISBN 1-891400-34-7

Living with Grief: a guide for year first year of grieving by Pamela D. Blair, Ph.D. and Brook Noel ($8.95) adapted from *I Wasn't Ready to Say Goodbye: Surviving, Coping and Healing After the Sudden Death of a Loved One* ISBN 1-891400-08-8

Surviving Holidays, Birthdays and Anniversaries: A Guide for Grieving During Special Occasions by Brook Noel ($8.95) ISBN 1-891400-03-7

You're Not Alone: Resources to Help You On Your Grief Journey by Brook Noel and Pamela D. Blair, Ph.D. ($9.95) ISBN 1-891400-63-0

Understanding the Emotional and Physical Effects of Grief by Brook Noel ($9.95) ISBN 1-891400-77-0

Finding Peace: Exercises to Help Heal the Pain of Loss by Brook Noel and Pamela D. Blair, Ph.D. ($9.95) ISBN 1-891400-78-9

My World is Upside Down: Making Sense of Life After Confronting Death by Brook Noel and Pamela D. Blair, Ph.D. ($9.95) ISBN 1-891400-24-X